Delight

Delighting in God can lift your spirits and calm your soul. While the coming days ahead are sure to have many ups and downs, your goal is to concentrate on His faithfulness— even in the little details—and to share your unwavering, deep-seated happiness with everyone around you.

Start by thinking about some of the big dates, anniversaries, and celebrations you have coming up. How can you savor those moments and experience true delight in the Lord?

Journal ways to make those moments extra special for yourself and your loved ones.

Take delight in the Lord,
and He will give you your heart's desires.
PSALM 37:4 CSB

The LORD your God is among you, a warrior who saves.
He will rejoice over you with gladness. He will be quiet in His love.
He will delight in you with singing.
ZEPHANIAH 3:17 CSB

The steps of a good man are
ordered by the LORD, and He delights in his way.
Though he fall, he shall not be utterly cast down;
for the LORD upholds him with His hand.
PSALM 37:23-24 NKJV

Delight yourself in the LORD;
and I will cause you to ride on the high hills of the earth.

The sweetness of a...friend gives delight.
PROVERBS 27:9 NKJV

The prayer of the upright is His delight.

PROVERBS 15:8 NKJV

Your love must be real. Hate what is evil, and hold on
to what is good. Love each other like brothers and sisters.
Give each other more honor than you want for yourselves.
ROMANS 12:9-10 NCV

The LORD had done great things for us; we were joyful.
PSALM 126:3 CSB

We thank God for you in return
for all the joy we experience before our God because of you.
I THESSALONIANS 3:9 CSB

You reveal the path of life to me; in Your presence is abundant joy.
PSALM 16:11 CSB

A joyful heart makes a face cheerful.
PROVERBS 15:13 CSB

God...provides us with all things to enjoy.
I TIMOTHY 6:17 CSB

May the God of hope fill you with all joy and peace.
ROMANS 15:13 CSB

A joyful heart is good medicine.
PROVERBS 17:22 CSB

God has chosen you...
He has set you apart with much joy.
PSALM 45:7 NCV

When you have many kinds of troubles, you should be full of joy,
because you know that these troubles test your faith,
and this will give you patience.
JAMES 1:2, 3 NCV

The LORD has filled my heart with joy.

I SAMUEL 2:1 NCV

Ask and you will receive, so that your joy
will be the fullest possible joy.
JOHN 16:24 NCV

Celebrate with great joy.

NEHEMIAH 8:12 NCV

You have put gladness in my heart.
PSALM 4:7 NKJV

The LORD takes pleasure in His people.
PSALM 149:4 NKJV

Every man should eat and drink
and enjoy the good of all his labor—it is the gift of God.
ECCLESIASTES 3:13 NKJV

Taste and see that the LORD is good.
How happy is the person who takes refuge in Him!
PSALM 34:8 CSB

Be happy with those who are happy.
ROMANS 12:15 NCV

The truly happy people are those who carefully study God's perfect law that makes people free, and they continue to study it. They do not forget what they heard, but they obey what God's teaching says. Those who do this will be made happy.

JAMES 1:25 NCV

Happy are those who...love the LORD'S teachings, and they think about those teachings day and night. They are strong, like a tree planted by a river. The tree produces fruit in season, and its leaves don't die. Everything they do will succeed.

PSALM 1:1, 2-3 NCV

Happy are those whose strength comes from You.

Made in the USA
Middletown, DE
25 January 2019